Character-Building—
Thought Power

Character-Building—
Thought Power

Ralph Waldo Trine

STONEWELL PRESS

ISBN 978-1-62730-005-6

Published by Stonewell Press, Salt Lake City, Utah.

Stonewell Press™ and the Stonewell Press logo are trademarks of Stonewell Press.

www.stonewellpress.com
editor@stonewellpress.com

Unconsciously we are forming habits every moment of our lives. Some are habits of a desirable nature; some are those of a most undesirable nature. Some, though not so bad in themselves, are exceedingly bad in their cumulative effects, and cause us at times much loss, much pain and anguish, while their opposites would, on the contrary, bring as much peace and joy, as well as a continually increasing power. Have we it within our power to determine at all times what types of habits shall take form in our lives? In other words, is habit-forming, character-building, a matter of mere chance, or have we it within our own control? We have, entirely and absolutely. "I will be what I will to be," can be said and should be said by every human soul.

After this has been bravely and determinedly said, and not only said, but fully inwardly realized, something yet remains. Something remains to be said regarding the great law underlying habit-forming, character-building; for there is a simple, natural, and thoroughly scientific method that all should know. A method whereby old, undesirable, earth-binding habits can be broken, and new, desirable, heaven-lifting habits can be acquired, a method whereby life in part or in its totality can be changed, provided one is sufficiently in earnest to know and, knowing it, to apply the law.

Thought is the force underlying all. And what do we mean by this? Simply this: Your every act—every conscious act—is preceded by a thought. Your dominating thoughts determine your dominating actions. In the realm of our own minds we have absolute control, or we should have, and if at any time we have not, then there is a method by which we can gain control, and in the realm of the mind become thorough masters. In order to get to the very foundation of the matter, let us look to this for a moment. For if thought is always parent to our acts, habits, character, life, then it is first necessary that we know fully how to control our thoughts.

Here let us refer to that law of the mind which is the same as is the law in connection with the reflex nerve system of the body, the law which says that whenever one does a certain thing in a certain way it is easier to do the same thing in the same way the next time, and still easier the next, and the next, and the next, until in time it comes to pass that no effort is required, or no effort worth speaking of; but on the opposite would require the effort. The mind carries with it the power that perpetuates its own type of thought, the same as the body carries with it through the reflex nerve system the power which perpetuates and makes continually easier its own particular acts. Thus a simple effort to control one's thoughts, a simple setting about it, even if at first failure is the result, and even if for a time failure seems to be about the only result, will in time, sooner or later, bring him to the point of easy, full, and complete control. Each one, then, can grow the power of determining, controlling his thought, the power of determining what types of thought he shall and what types he shall not entertain. For let us never part in mind with this fact, that every earnest effort along any line makes the end aimed at just a little easier for each succeeding effort, even if, as has been said, apparent failure is the result of the earlier efforts. This is a case where even failure is success, for the failure is not in the effort, and every earnest effort adds an increment of power that will eventually accomplish the end aimed at. We can, then, gain the full and complete power of determining what character, what type of thoughts we entertain.

Shall we now give attention to some two or three concrete cases? Here is a man, the cashier of a large mercantile establishment, or cashier of a bank. In his morning paper he reads of a man who has become suddenly rich, has made a fortune of half a million or a million dollars in a few hours through speculation on the stock market. Perhaps he has seen an account of another man who has done practically the same thing lately. He is not quite wise enough, however, to comprehend the fact that when he reads of one or two cases of this kind he could find, were he to look into the matter carefully, one or two hundred cases of men who have lost all they had in the same way.

He thinks, however, that he will be one of the fortunate ones. He does not fully realize that there are no short cuts to wealth honestly made. He takes a part of his savings, and as is true in practically all cases of this kind, he loses all that he has put in, Thinking now that he sees why he lost, and that had he more money he would be able to get back what he has lost, and perhaps make a handsome sum in addition, and make it quickly, the thought comes to him to use some of the funds he has charge of. In nine cases out of ten, if not ten cases in every ten, the results that inevitably follow this are known sufficiently well to make it unnecessary to follow him farther.

Where is the man's safety in the light of what we have been considering? Simply this: the moment the thought of using for his own purpose funds belonging to others enters his mind, if he is wise he will instantly put the thought from his mind. If he is a fool he will entertain it. In the degree in which he entertains it, it will grow upon him; it will become the absorbing thought in his mind; it will finally become master of his will power, and through rapidly succeeding steps, dishonor, shame, degradation, penitentiary, remorse will be his. It is easy for him to put the thought from his mind when it first enters; but as he entertains it, it grows into such proportions that it becomes more and more difficult for him to put it from his mind; and by and by it becomes practically impossible for him to do it. The light of the match, which but a little effort of the breath would have extinguished at first, has imparted a flame that is raging through the entire building, and now it is almost if not quite impossible to conquer it.

Shall we notice another concrete case? A trite case, perhaps, but one in which we can see how habit is formed, and also how the same habit can be unformed. Here is a young man, he may be the son of poor parents, or he may be the son of rich parents; one in the ordinary ranks of life, or one of high social standing, whatever that means. He is good hearted, one of good impulses generally speaking, a good fellow. He is out with some companions, companions of the same general type. They are out for a pleasant evening, out for a good time. They are apt at times to be thoughtless, even careless. The suggestion is made by one of the company, not that they get drunk, no, not at all; but merely that they go and have something to drink together. The young man whom we first mentioned, wanting to be genial, scarcely listens to the suggestion that comes into his inner consciousness that it will be better for him not to fall in with the others in this. He does not stop long enough to realize the fact that the greatest strength and nobility of character lies always in taking a firm stand on the aide of the right, and allow himself to be influenced by nothing that will weaken this stand. He goes, therefore, with his companions to the drinking place. With the same or with other companions this is repeated now and then; and each time it is repeated his power of saying "No" is gradually decreasing. In this way he has grown a little liking for intoxicants, and takes them perhaps now and then by himself.

He does not dream, or in the slightest degree realize, what way he is tending, until there comes a day when he awakens to the consciousness of the fact that he hasn't the power nor even the impulse to resist the taste which has gradually grown into a minor form of craving for intoxicants. Thinking, however, that he will be able to stop when he is really in danger of getting into the drink habit, he goes thoughtlessly and carelessly on. We will pass over the various intervening steps and come to the time when we find him a confirmed drunkard. It is simply the same old story told a thousand or even a million times over.

He finally awakens to his true condition; and through the shame, the anguish, the degradation, and the want that comes upon him he longs for a return of the days when he was a free man. But hope has almost gone from his life. It would have been easier for him never to have begun, and easier for him to have stopped before he reached his present condition; but even in his present condition, be it the lowest and the most helpless and hopeless that can be imagined, he has the power to get out of it and be a free man once again. Let us see. The desire for drink comes upon him again. If he entertains the thought, the desire, he is lost again. His only hope, his only means of escape is this: the moment, aye, the very instant the thought comes to him, if he will put it out of his mind he will thereby put out the little flame of the match. If he entertains the thought the little flame will communicate itself until almost before he is aware of it a consuming fire is raging, and then effort is almost useless. The thought must be banished from the mind the instant it enters; dalliance with it means failure and defeat, or a fight that will be indescribably fiercer than it would be if the thought is ejected at the beginning.

And here we must say a word regarding a certain great law that we may call the "law of indirectness." A thought can be put out of the mind easier and more successfully, not by dwelling upon it, not by, attempting to put it out directly, but by throwing the mind on to some other object by putting some other object of thought into the mind. This may be, for example, the ideal of full and perfect self-mastery, or it may be something of a nature entirely distinct from the thought which presents itself, something to which the mind goes easily and naturally. This will in time become the absorbing thought in the mind, and the danger is past. This same course of action repeated will gradually grow the power of putting more readily out of mind the thought of drink as it presents itself, and will gradually grow the power of putting into the mind those objects of thought one most desires. The result will be that as time passes the thought of drink will present itself less and less, and when it does present itself it can be put out of the mind more easily each succeeding time, until the time comes when it can be put out without difficulty, and eventually the time will come when the thought will enter the mind no more at all.

Still another case. You may be more or less of an irritable nature naturally, perhaps, provoked easily to anger. Someone says something or does something that you dislike, and your first impulse is to show resentment and possibly to give way to anger. In the degree that you allow this resentment to display itself, that you allow yourself to give way to anger, in that degree will it become easier to do the same thing when any cause, even a very slight cause, presents itself. It will, moreover, become continually harder for you to refrain from it, until resentment, anger, and possibly even hatred and revenge become characteristics of your nature, robbing it of its sunniness, its charm, and its brightness for all with whom you come in contact.

If, however, the instant the impulse to resentment and anger arises, you check it then and there, and throw the mind on to some other object of thought, the power will gradually grow itself of doing this same thing more readily, more easily, as succeeding like causes present themselves, until by and by the time will come when there will be scarcely anything that can irritate you, and nothing that can impel you to anger; until by and by a matchless brightness and charm of nature and disposition will become habitually yours, a brightness and charm you would scarcely think possible today. And so we might take up case after case, characteristic after characteristic, habit after habit. The habit of faultfinding and its opposite are grown in identically the same way; the characteristic of jealousy and its opposite; the characteristic of fear and its opposite. In this same way we grow either love or hatred; in this way we come to take a gloomy, pessimistic view of life, which objectifies itself in a nature, a disposition of this type, or we grow that sunny, hopeful, cheerful, buoyant nature that brings with it so much joy and beauty and power for ourselves, as well as so much hope and inspiration and joy for all the world.

There is nothing more true in connection with human life than that we grow into the likeness of those things we contemplate. Literally and scientifically and necessarily true is it that "as a man thinketh in his heart, so is he." The "is" part is his character. His character is the sum total of his habits. His habits have been formed by· his conscious acts; but every conscious act is, as we have found, preceded by a thought. And so we have it—thought on the one hand, character, life, and destiny on the other. And simple it becomes when we bear in mind that it is simply the thought of the present moment, and the next moment when it is upon us, and then the next, and so on through all time.

One can in this way attain to whatever ideals he would attain to. Two steps are necessary: first, as the days pass, to form one's ideals; and second, to follow them continually, whatever may arise, wherever they may lead him. Always remember that the great and strong character is the one who is ever ready to sacrifice the present pleasure for the future good. He who will thus follow his highest ideals as they present themselves to him day after day, year after year, will find that as Dante, following his beloved from world to world, finally found her at the gates of Paradise, so he will find himself eventually at the same gates. Life is not, we may say, for mere passing pleasure, but for the highest unfoldment that one can attain to, the noblest character that one can grow, and for the greatest service that one can render to all mankind. In this, however, we will find the highest pleasure, for in this the only real pleasure lies. He who would find it by any short cuts, or by entering upon any other paths, will inevitably find that his last state is always worse than his first; and if he proceed upon paths other than these he will find that he will never find real and lasting pleasure at all.

The question is not, "What are the conditions in our lives?" but, "How do we meet the conditions that we find there?" And whatever the conditions are, it is unwise and profitless to look upon them, even if they are conditions that we would have otherwise, in the attitude of complaint, for complaint will bring depression, and depression will weaken and possibly even kill the spirit that would engender the power that would enable us to bring into our lives an entirely new set of conditions.

In order to be concrete, even at the risk of being personal, I will say that in my own experience there have come at various times into my life circumstances and conditions that I gladly would have run from at the time—conditions that caused at the time humiliation and shame and anguish of spirit. But invariably, as sufficient time has passed, I have been able to look back and see clearly the part that every experience of the type just mentioned had to play in my life. I have seen the lessons it was essential for me to learn; and the result is that now I would not drop a single one of these experiences from my life, humiliating and hard to bear as they were at the time; no, not for the world. And here is also a lesson I have learned: whatever conditions are in my life today that are not the easiest and most agreeable, and whatever conditions of this type all coming time may bring, I will take them just as they come, without complaint, without depression, and meet them in the wisest possible way; knowing that they are the best possible conditions that could be in my life at the time, or otherwise they would not be there; realizing the fact that, although I may not at the time see why they are in my life, although I may not see just what part they have to play, the time will come, and when it comes I will see it all, and thank God for every condition just as it came.

Each one is so apt to think that his own conditions, his own trials or troubles or sorrows, or his own struggles, as the case may be, are greater than those of the great mass of mankind, or possibly greater than those of any one else in the world. He forgets that each one has his own peculiar trials or troubles or sorrows to bear, or struggles in habits to overcome, and that his is but the common lot of all the human race. We are apt to make the mistake in this—in that we see and feel keenly our own trials, or adverse conditions, or characteristics to be overcome, while those of others we do not see so clearly, and hence we are apt to think that they are not at all equal to our own. Each has his own problems to work out. Each must work out his own problems. Each must grow the insight that will enable him to see what the causes are that have brought the unfavorable conditions into his life; each must grow the strength that will enable him to face these conditions, and to set into operation forces that will bring about a different set of conditions. We may be of aid to one another by way of suggestion, by way of bringing to one another a knowledge of certain higher laws and forces—laws and forces that will make it easier to do that which we would do. The doing, however, must be done by each one for himself. And so the way to get out of any conditioning we have got into, either knowingly or inadvertently, either intentionally or unintentionally, is to take time to look the conditions squarely in the face, and to find the law whereby they have come about. And when we have discovered the law, the thing to do is not to rebel against it, not to resist it, but to go with it by working in harmony with it. If we work in harmony with it, it will work for our highest good, and will take us wheresoever we desire. If we oppose it, if we resist it, if we fail to work in harmony with it, it will eventually break us to pieces. The law is immutable in its workings. Go with it, and it brings all things our way; resist it, and it brings suffering, pain, loss, and desolation.

But a few days ago I was talking with a lady, a most estimable lady living on a little New England farm of some five or six acres. Her husband died a few years ago, a good-hearted, industrious man, but one who spent practically all of his earnings in drink. When he died the little farm was unpaid for, and the wife found herself without any visible means of support, with a family of several to care for. Instead of being discouraged with what many would have called her hard lot, instead of rebelling against the circumstances in which she found herself, she faced the matter bravely, firmly believing that there were ways by which she could manage, though she could not see them clearly at the time. She took up her burden where she found it, and went bravely forward. For several years she has been taking care of summer boarders who come to that part of the country, getting up regularly, she told me, at from half-past three to four o'clock in the morning, and working until ten o'clock each night. In the winter time, when this means of revenue is cut off, she has gone out to do nursing in the country round about. In this way the little farm is now almost paid for; her children have been kept in school, and they are now able to aid her to a greater or less extent. Through it all she has entertained no fears nor forebodings; she has shown no rebellion of any kind. She has not kicked against the circumstances which brought about the conditions in which she found herself, but she has put herself into harmony with the law that would bring her into another set of conditions. And through it all, she told me, she has been continually grateful that she has been able to work, and that whatever her own circumstances have been, she has never yet failed to find some one whose circumstances were still a little worse than hers, and for whom it was possible for her to render some little service.

Most heartily she appreciates the fact, and most grateful is she for it, that the little home is now almost paid for, and soon no more of her earnings will have to go out in that channel. The dear little home, she said, would be all the more precious to her by virtue of the fact that it was finally hers through her own efforts. The strength and nobility of character that have come to her during these years, the sweetness of disposition, the sympathy and care for others, her faith in the final triumph of all that is honest and true and pure and good, are qualities that thousands and hundreds of thousands of women, yes, of both men and women, who are apparently in better circumstances in life, can justly envy. And should the little farm home be taken away tomorrow, she has gained something that a farm of a thousand acres could not buy. By going about her work in the way she has gone about it the burden of it all has been lightened, and her work has been made truly enjoyable.

Let us take a moment to see how these same conditions would have been met by a person of less wisdom, one not so far-sighted as this dear, good woman has been. For a time possibly her spirit would have been crushed. Fears and forebodings of all kinds would probably have taken hold of her, and she would have felt that nothing that she could do would be of any avail. Or she might have rebelled against the agencies, against the law which brought about the conditions in which she found herself, and she might have become embittered against the world, and gradually also against the various people with whom she came in contact. Or again, she might have thought that her efforts would be unable to meet the circumstances, and that it was the duty of someone to lift her out of her difficulties. In this way no progress at all would have been made towards the accomplishment of the desired results, and continually she would have felt more keenly the circumstances in which she found herself, because there was nothing else to occupy her mind. In this way the little farm would not have become hers, she would not have been able to do anything for others, and her nature would have become embittered against everything and everybody.

True it is, then, not, "What are the conditions in one's life?" but, "How does he meet the conditions that he finds there?" This will determine all. And if at any time we are apt to think that our own lot is about the hardest there is, and if we are able at any time to persuade ourselves that we can find no one whose lot is just a little harder than ours, let us then study for a little while the character Pompilia, in Browning's poem and after studying it, thank God that the conditions in our life are so favorable; and then set about with a trusting and intrepid spirit to actualize the conditions that we most desire.

Thought is at the bottom of all progress or retrogression, of all success or failure, of all that is desirable or undesirable in human life. The type of thought we entertain both creates and draws conditions that crystallize about it, conditions exactly the same in nature as is the thought that gives them form. Thoughts are forces, and each creates of its kind, whether we realize it or not. The great law of the drawing power of the mind, which says that like creates like, and that like attracts like, is continually working in every human life, for it is one of the great immutable laws of the universe. For one to take time to see clearly the things he would attain to, and then to hold that ideal steadily and continually before his mind, never allowing faith—his positive thought-forces—to give way to or to be neutralized by doubts and fears, and then to set about doing each day what his hands find to do, never complaining, but spending the time that he would otherwise spend in complaint in focusing his thought-forces upon the ideal that his mind has built, will sooner or later bring about the full materialization of that for which he sets out. There are those who, when they begin to grasp the fact that there is what we may term a "science of thought," who, when they begin to realize that through the instrumentality of our interior, spiritual, thought-forces we have the power of gradually molding the everyday conditions of life as we would have them, in their early enthusiasm are not able to see results as quickly as they expect and are apt to think, therefore, that after all there is not very much in that which has but newly come to their knowledge. They must remember, however, that in endeavoring to overcome an old habit or to grow a new habit, everything cannot be done all at once.

In the degree that we attempt to use the thought-forces do we continually become able to use them more effectively. Progress is slow at first, more rapid as we proceed. Power grows by using, or, in other words, using brings a continually increasing power. This is governed by law the same as are all things in our lives, and all things in the universe about us. Every act and advancement made by the musician is in full accordance with law. No one commencing the study of music can, for example, sit down to the piano and play the piece of a master at the first effort. He must not conclude, however, nor does he conclude, that the piece of the master cannot be played by him, or, for that matter, by anyone. He begins to practice the piece. The law of the mind that we have already noticed comes to his aid, whereby his mind follows the music more readily, more rapidly, and more surely each succeeding time, and there also comes into operation and to his aid the law underlying the action of the reflex nerve system of the body, which we have also noticed, whereby his fingers coordinate their movements with the movements of his mind more readily, more rapidly, and more accurately each succeeding time; until by and by the time comes when that which he stumbles through at first, that in which there is no harmony, nothing but discord, finally reveals itself as the music of the master, the music that thrills and moves masses of men and women. So it is in the use of the thought-forces.

It is the reiteration, the constant reiteration of the thought that grows the power of continually stronger thought-focusing, and that finally brings manifestation.

There is character-building not only for the young but for the old as well. And what a difference there is in elderly people! How many grow old gracefully, and how many grow old in ways of quite a different nature. There is a sweetness and charm that combine for attractiveness in old age the same as there is something that cannot be described by these words. Some grow continually more dear to their friends and to the members of their immediate households, while others become possessed of the idea that their friends and the members of their households have less of a regard for them than they formerly had, and many times they are not far wrong. The one continually sees more in life to enjoy, the other sees continually less. The one becomes more dear and attractive to others, the other less so. And why is this? Through chance? By no means. Personally I do not believe there is any such thing as chance in the whole of human life, nor even in the world or the great universe in which we live. The one great law of cause and effect is absolute; and effect is always kindred to its own peculiar cause, although we may have at times to go back considerably farther than we are accustomed to in order to find the cause, the parent of this or that effect, or actualized, though not necessarily permanently actualized, condition.

Why, then, the vast difference in the two types of

elderly people? The one keeps from worryings, and fearings, and frettings, and foundationless imaginings, while the other seems especially to cultivate these, to give himself or herself especially to them. And why is this? At a certain time in life, differing somewhat in different people, life-long mental states, habits, and characteristics begin to focus themselves and come to the surface, so to speak. Predominating thoughts and mental states begin to show themselves in actualized qualities and characteristics as never before, and no one is immune.

In the lane leading to the orchard is a tree. For years it has been growing only "natural fruit." Not long since it was grafted upon. The spring has come and gone. One-half of the tree was in bloom and the other half also. The blossoms on each part could not be distinguished by the casual observer. The blossoms have been followed by young fruit which hangs abundantly on the entire tree. There is but a slight difference in it now; but a few weeks later the difference in form, in size, in color, in flavor, in keeping qualities, will be so marked that no one can fail to tell them apart or have difficulty in choosing between them. The one will be a small, somewhat hard and gnarled, tart, yellowish-green apple, and will keep but a few weeks into the fall of the year. The other will be a large, delicately flavored apple, mellow, deep red in color, and will keep until the tree which bore it is in bloom again.

But why this incident from nature's garden? Up to a certain period in the fruit's growth, although the interior, forming qualities of the apples were slightly different from the beginning, there was but little to distinguish them. At a certain period in their growth, however, their differing interior qualities began to externalize themselves so rapidly and so markedly that the two fruits became of such a vastly different type that, as we have seen, no one could hesitate in choosing between them. And knowing once the soul, the forming, the determining qualities of each, we can thereafter tell beforehand with a certainty that is quite absolute what it, the externalized product of each portion of the tree, will be.

And it is quite the same in human life. If one would have a beautiful and attractive old age, he must begin it in youth and in middle life. If, however, he has neglected or failed in this, he can then wisely adapt himself to circumstances and give himself zealously to putting into operation all necessary counterbalancing forces and influences. Where there is life nothing is ever irretrievably lost, though the enjoyment of the higher good may be long delayed. But if one would have an especially beautiful and attractive old age he must begin it in early and in middle life, for there comes by and by a sort of "rounding-up" process when long-lived-in habits of thought begin to take unto themselves a strongly dominating power, and the thought habits of a lifetime begin to come to the surface.

Fear and worry, selfishness, a hard-fisted, grabbing, holding disposition, a carping, fault-finding, nagging tendency, a slavery of thought and action to the think-

ing or to the opinions of others, a lacking of consid-
eration, thought, and sympathy for others, a lack of
charity for the thoughts, the motives, and the acts
of others, a lack of knowledge of the powerful and
inevitable building qualities of thought, as well as a
lack of faith in the eternal goodness and love and
power of the Source of our being, all combine in
time to make the old age of those in whom they find
life, that barren, cheerless, unwelcome something,
unattractive or even repellent to itself as well as to
others, that we not infrequently find, while their opposites, on the contrary, combine, and seem to be
helped on by heavenly agencies, to bring about that
cheerful, hopeful, helpful, beautified, and hallowed
old age that is so welcome and so attractive both to
itself and to all with whom it comes in contact. Both
types of thoughts, qualities, and dispositions, moreover, externalize themselves in the voice, in the pe-
culiarly different ways in which they mark the face,
in the stoop or lack of stoop in the form, as also in
the healthy or unhealthy conditions of the mind and
body, and their susceptibility to disorders and weak-
nesses of various kinds.

It is not a bad thing for each one early to get a little
"philosophy" into his life. It will be of much aid as he
advances in life; it will many times be a source of
great comfort, as well as of strength, in trying times
and in later life. We may even, though gently perhaps, make sport of the one who has his little philosophy, but unless we have something similar the time
will come when the very lack of it will deride us. It

may be at times, though not necessarily, that the one who has it is not always so successful in affairs when it comes to a purely money or business success, but it supplies many times a very real something in life that the one of money or business success only is starving for, though he doesn't know what the real lack is, and although he hasn't money enough in all the world to buy it did he know.

It is well to find our centre early, and if not early then late; but, late or early, the thing to do is to find it. While we are in life the one essential thing is to play our part bravely and well and to keep our active interest in all its varying phases, the same as it is well to be able to adapt ourselves always to changing conditions. It is by the winds of heaven blowing over it continually and keeping it in constant motion, or by its continual onward movement, that the water in pool or stream is kept sweet and clear, for otherwise it would become stagnant and covered with slime. If we are attractive or unattractive to ourselves and to others the cause lies in ourselves; this is true of all ages, and it is well for us, young or old, to recognize it. It is well, other things being equal, to adapt ourselves to those about us, but it is hardly fair for the old to think that all the adapting should be on the part of the young, with no kindred duty on their part. Many times old-age loses much of its attractiveness on account of a peculiar notion of this kind. The principle of reciprocity must hold in all ages in life, and whatever the age, if we fail to observe it, it results always sooner or later in our own undoing.

We are all in Life's great play—comedy and tragedy, smiles and tears, sunshine and shadow, summer and winter, and in time we take all parts. We must take our part, whatever it may be, at any given time, always bravely and with a keen appreciation of every opportunity, and a keen alertness at every turn as the play progresses. A good "entrance" and a good "exit" contribute strongly to the playing of a deservedly worthy role. We are not always able perhaps to choose just as we would the details of our entrance, but the manner of our playing and the manner of our exit we can all determine, and this no man, no power can deny us; this in every human life can be made indeed most glorious, however humble it may begin, or however humble it may remain or exalted it may become, according to conventional standards of judgment.

To me we are here for divine self-realization through experience. We progress in the degree that we manipulate wisely all things that enter into our lives, and that make the sum total of each one's life experience. Let us be brave and strong in the presence of each problem as it presents itself and make the best of all. Let us help the things we can help, and let us be not bothered or crippled by the things we cannot help. The great God of all is watching and manipulating these things most wisely and we need not fear or even have concern regarding them.

To live to our highest in all things that pertain to us, to lend a hand as best we can to all others for this same end, to aid in righting the wrongs that cross our path by means of pointing the wrongdoer to a better way, and thus aiding him in becoming a power for good, to remain in nature always sweet and simple and humble, and therefore strong, to open ourselves fully and to keep ourselves as fit channels for the Divine Power to work through us, to open ourselves, and to keep our faces always to the light, to love all things and to stand in awe or fear of nothing save our own wrong-doing, to recognize the good lying at the heart of all things, waiting for expression all in its own good way and time—this will make our part in life's great and as yet not fully understood play truly glorious, and we need then stand in fear of nothing, life nor death, for death is life. Or rather, it is the quick transition to life in another form; the putting off of the old coat and the putting on of a new; the falling away of the material body and the taking of the soul to itself a new and finer body, better adapted to its needs and surroundings in another world of experience and growth and still greater divine self-realization; a going out with all that it has gained of this nature in this world, but with no possessions material; a passing not from light to darkness, but from light to light; a taking up of life in another from just where we leave it off here; an experience not to be shunned or dreaded or feared, but to be welcomed when it comes in its own good way and time.

All life is from within out. This is something that cannot be reiterated too often. The springs of life are all from within. This being true, it would be well for us to give more time to the inner life than we are accustomed to give to it, especially in this Western world.

There is nothing that will bring us such abundant returns as to take a little time in the quiet each day of our lives. We need this to get the kinks out of our minds, and hence out of our lives. We need this to form better the higher ideals of life. We need this in order to see clearly in mind the things upon which we would concentrate and focus the thought-forces. We need this in order to make continually anew and to keep our conscious connection with the Infinite. We need this in order that the rush and hurry of our everyday life does not keep us away from the conscious realization of the fact that the spirit of Infinite life and power that is back of all, working in and through all, the life of all, is the life of our life, and the source of our power; and that outside of this we have no life and we have no power. To realize this fact fully, and to live in it consciously at all times, is to find the kingdom of God, which is essentially an inner kingdom, and can never be anything else. The kingdom of heaven is to be found only within, and this is done once for all, and in a manner in which it cannot otherwise be done, when we come into the conscious, living realization of the fact that in our real selves we are essentially one with the Divine life, and open ourselves continually so that this Divine life can speak to and manifest through us. In this way we come into the condition where we are continually walking with God. In this way the consciousness of God becomes a living reality in our lives; and in the degree in which it becomes a reality does it bring us into the realization of continually increasing wisdom, insight, and power. This consciousness of God in the soul of man is the essence, indeed, the sum and substance, of all religion. This identifies religion with every act and every moment of everyday life. That which does not identify itself with every moment of every day and with every act of life is religion in name only and not in reality. This consciousness of God in the soul of man is the one thing uniformly taught by all the prophets, by all the inspired ones, by all the seers and mystics in the world's history, whatever the time, wherever the country, whatever the religion, whatever minor differences we may find in their lives and teachings. In regard to this they all agree; indeed, this is the essence of their teaching, as it has also been the secret of their power and the secret of their lasting influence.

It is the attitude of the child that is necessary before we can enter into the kingdom of heaven. As it was said, "Except ye become as little children, ye cannot enter into the kingdom of heaven." For we then realize that of ourselves we can do nothing, but that it is only as we realize that it is the Divine life and power working within us, and it is only as we open ourselves that it may work through us, that we are or can do anything. It is thus that the simple life, which is essentially the life of the greatest enjoyment and the greatest attainment, is entered upon.

In the Orient the people as a class take far more time in the quiet, in the silence, than we take. Some of them carry this possibly to as great an extreme as we carry the opposite, with the result that they do not actualize and objectify in the outer life the things they dream in the inner life. We give so much time to the activities of the outer life that we do not take sufficient time in the quiet to form in the inner, spiritual, thought-life the ideals and the conditions that we would have actualized and manifested in the outer life. The result is that we take life in a kind of haphazard way, taking it as it comes, thinking not very much about it until, perhaps, pushed by some bitter experiences, instead of molding it, through the agency of the inner forces, exactly as we would have it. We need to strike the happy balance between the custom in this respect of the Eastern and Western worlds, and go to the extreme of neither the one nor the other. This alone will give the ideal life; and it is the ideal life only that is the thoroughly satisfactory life. In the Orient there are many who are day after day sitting in the quiet, meditating, contemplating, idealizing, with their eyes focused on their stomachs in spiritual reverie, while through lack of outer activities, in their stomachs, they are actually starving. In this Western world, men and women, in the rush and activity of our accustomed life, are running hither and thither, with no centre, no foundation upon which to stand, nothing to which they can anchor their lives, because they do not take sufficient time to come into the realization of what the centre, of what the reality of their lives is.

If the Oriental would do his contemplating, and

then get up and do his work, he would be in a better condition; he would be living a more normal and satisfactory life. If we in the Occident would take more time from the rush and activity of life for contemplation, for meditation, for idealization, for becoming acquainted with our real selves, and then go about our work manifesting the powers of our real selves, we would be far better off, because we would be living a more natural, a more normal life. To find one's centre, to become centred in the Infinite, is the first great essential of every satisfactory life; and then to go out, thinking, speaking, working, loving, living, from this centre.

In the highest character-building, such as we have been considering, there are those who feel they are handicapped by what we term heredity. In a sense they are right; in another sense they are totally wrong. It is along the same lines as the thought which many before us had inculcated in them through the couplet in the New England Primer: "In Adam's fall, we sinned all." Now, in the first place, it is rather hard to understand the justice of this if it is true. In the second place, it is rather hard to understand why it is true. And in the third place there is no truth in it at all. We are now dealing with the real essential self, and, however old Adam is, God is eternal. This means you; it means me; it means every human soul. When we fully realize this fact we see that heredity is a reed that is easily broken. The life of every one is in his own hands and he can make it in character, in attainment, in power, in divine self-realization, and hence in influence, exactly what he wills to make it. All things that he most fondly dreams of are his, or may become so if he is truly in earnest; and as he rises more and more to his ideal, and grows in the strength and influence of his character, he becomes an example and an inspiration to all with whom he comes in contact; so that through him the weak and faltering are encouraged and strengthened; so that those of low ideals and of a low type of life instinctively and inevitably have their ideals raised, and the ideals of no one can be raised without its showing forth in his outer life. As he advances in his grasp upon and understanding of the power and potency of the thought-forces, he finds that many times through the process of mental suggestion he can be of tremendous aid to one who is weak and struggling, by sending him now and then, and by continually holding him in, the highest thought, in the thought of the highest strength, wisdom and love. The power of "suggestion," mental suggestion, is one that has tremendous possibilities for good if we will but study into it carefully, understand it fully, and use it rightly.

The one who takes sufficient time in the quiet mentally to form his ideals, sufficient time to make and to keep continually his conscious connection with the Infinite, with the Divine life and forces, is the one who is best adapted to the strenuous life. He it is who can go out and deal, with sagacity and power, with whatever issues may arise in the affairs of everyday life. He it is who is building not for the years but for the centuries; not for time, but for the eternities. And he can go out knowing not whither he goes, knowing that the Divine life within him will never fail him, but will lead him on until he beholds the Father face to face.

He is building for the centuries because only that which is the highest, the truest, the noblest, and best will abide the test of the centuries. He is building for eternity because when the transition we call death takes place, life, character, self-mastery, divine self-realization—the only things that the soul when stripped of everything else takes with it—he has in abundance, in life, or when the time of the transition to another form of life comes, he is never afraid, never fearful, because he knows and realizes that behind him, within him, beyond him, is the Infinite wisdom and love; and in this he is eternally centred, and from it he can never be separated. With Whittier he sings:

> I know not where His islands lift
> Their fronded palms in air;
> I only know I cannot drift
> Beyond His love and care